Content

2 Introduction

SWEATER BASICS
3 Gauge
4 Size
4 Schematics
5 Blocking
5 Assembly
6 Seaming
9 Picking Up Stitches

SWEATERS
10 Cable-Rib Pullover
12 Textured V-Neck Sweater
14 Raglan Turtleneck Sweater
16 Honeycomb Sweater
19 Striped Boat-Neck Sweater
22 Twists and Cables Sweater
25 Off-Center Cable Sweater
28 Bulky Garter Sweater
30 Classic Raglan Sweater
33 Hooded or Turtleneck Sweater
36 Perforated Ridges Sweater
38 Chevron Sweater

INTRODUCTION

Whether you're a newer knitter looking to make your first sweater or a seasoned knitter in search of that next special design, Sweaters 101 is the booklet for you.

For those just delving into the thrill of knitting sweaters, you'll find vital information that will guide you every step of the way. Gauge, construction, seaming, and finishing are all explained in a concise and straightforward manner, giving you the core knowledge needed to move forward with confidence.

For knitters of all skill levels, this booklet contains 12 beautiful sweater patterns. Chosen for their diverse and appealing designs, these sweaters also feature simple constructions and finishing. With patterns that include eyelets, stripes, cables, textural stitches, as well as varying silhouettes and necklines, you'll find multiple patterns that you will enjoy knitting and can't wait to wear.

Sweaters are one of the most classic projects a knitter can make, and it's no wonder why. Hand-knit sweaters are functional and fashionable. Knit well and handled with care, they can keep you cozy for years to come. So, start a sweater today and begin a knitting journey that is worth every stitch.

SWEATER BASICS

GAUGE

One of the most important factors when knitting a sweater is gauge, meaning the number of rows and stitches per inch in your knitted fabric. Every pattern will list a specific gauge, and if your knitting does not match that gauge then your sweater might not be the right size.

To make sure you have the correct gauge, always make a gauge swatch before beginning your sweater. Using the appropriate yarn and needle size, cast on enough stitches to create a square at least 4"/10cm wide. Then work the specified stitch pattern until the swatch is a little more than 4"/10cm high. Once that is complete, bind off and lay down the swatch on a smooth, hard surface.

1) Using a tape measure or ruler, measure 4"/10cm horizontally across the swatch. Count the number of stitches in those 4"/10cm.

2) Place the tape measure or ruler vertically across the swatch and count the number of rows in those 4"/10cm.

As a general rule, larger needles give fewer stitches to the inch, smaller needles give more.

Compare the number of stitches and rows in your swatch to those in the gauge given for the pattern. If they match, you can start on your sweater. If they don't match, change your needle size and try again.

If there are **too few** stitches in the 4"/10cm of your swatch, try again using needles **1 or 2 sizes smaller**. If there are **too many** stitches, try again using needles **1 or 2 sizes larger**.

Try different needle sizes until you get the correct gauge. Once you have the correct gauge, you can start your sweater.

Here, each swatch was made in stockinette stitch with the same number of stitches and rows, but using three different needle sizes, from smaller to larger. The smaller the needle, the smaller the stitch; the larger the needle, the larger the stitch. As you can see, gauge can have a big effect.

SIZE

Most sweater patterns provide instructions for the smallest size, with larger sizes given in parentheses: S (M, L), for example. If the pattern says to cast on 43 (44, 46) sts, that means you would cast on 43 stitches for a size Small, 44 stitches for a size Medium, and 46 stitches for a size Large. To size yourself against a pattern, measure around the fullest part of your chest. As you measure, hold the tape snug, but not too tight, and be sure to measure accurately. Giving yourself a few inches more or less won't get you a garment that fits properly. Compare the bust/chest measurement in the pattern to your own measurements, remembering that the numbers given in the pattern refer to the finished size of the garment. Choose the size with the bust measurement that comes closest to your own.

> **TIP**
> Measure a sweater you like that is similar in style to the one shown in the pattern and use it as a guide for picking your size.

> **TIP**
> Before you begin the sweater, read through the pattern and highlight or circle the numbers that pertain to your size.

SCHEMATICS

Many sweater patterns include schematics, which are line illustrations, drawn to scale, that represent the various parts of the sweater. These are labeled with the name of the piece (back, front, sleeve) and measurements. The numbers preceding the parentheses are the measurements for the smallest size; those inside indicate measurements for sequentially increasing sizes.

Pay careful attention to how the lines along the side of the schematics are divided up and labeled, as that tells you how long each section of the piece should be. For example, on the SLEEVE you see that the ribbing should be 1½" long (for all sizes), the length from the ribbing to the underarm bind-offs should be 16 (16, 16½, 16½, 17)", and the length from the underarm bind-offs to the top of the sleeve should be 7¾ (8¼, 8¾, 9¼, 9¾)".

Schematics allow you to see the shape of each piece you are about to make. If you've followed the instructions correctly, your knit pieces will look like the picture when you've finished.

Schematics also help you to make sure the measurements of your finished knit pieces match those given in the pattern instructions. To see how your pieces are shaping up as you knit, lay the piece out on a flat, smooth surface and, using a tape measure, take the measurement in the middle of a row. Determine the length of your work by measuring from the row below your needle to the bottom edge. When measuring the length of an armhole, don't measure along the curve or slanted edge—if you do the measurement will be inaccurate. Instead, measure in a straight line from the needle to the first armhole decrease.

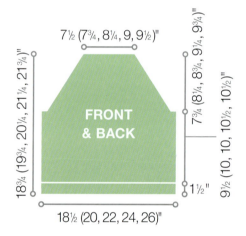

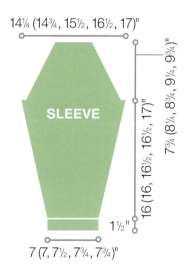

BLOCKING

Once you've finished knitting your pieces, the next step is to block them. This is one step that is tempting to skip, but don't. Blocking evens out your stitches and makes sure your project will be the correct size and shape. There are a couple of methods of blocking, but both produce the same result. To determine which method you should use with your yarn, consult the ball band or reference the blocking guide found below.

Wet Blocking

Immerse the piece in cool water and gently handwash the fabric to even out your stitches and settle them in place. Let the piece soak for a few minutes, then press out the water. Never wring out a knitted fabric. Fold it and squeeze out the excess water. Next, lay the piece on an ironing board or blocking mats, pin it to the appropriate size and shape, and let it dry. Rather than soaking, you may choose to first pin the piece into shape and then use a spray bottle to dampen the fabric. Once completely dry, the piece will keep the size and shape to which it was pinned.

Steam Blocking

First pin the piece to the appropriate size and shape. Then use a steamer or an iron to blast steam onto the piece. If using an iron, be sure to not let it touch the piece, simply hold it near. Once the piece is damp, smooth out any remaining bumps by hand and leave it to dry. Once completely dry, the piece will keep the size and shape to which it was pinned.

Blocking Guide

Angora	Wet block by spraying.
Cotton	Wet block or warm/hot steam block.
Linen	Wet block or warm/hot steam block.
Lurex	Do not block.
Mohair	Wet block by spraying.
Novelties	Do not block.
Synthetics	Carefully follow instructions on ball band—usually wet block by spraying. Do not press.
Wool and all wool-like fibers (alpaca, camel hair, cashmere)	Wet block by spraying or warm steam block.
Wool blends	Wet block by spraying. Do not steam unless tested.

ASSEMBLY

Once you have blocked your sweater pieces to the perfect sizes, it is time to put them together. Of course, there are many different ways to make a sweater, but for a sweater that consists of separate pieces for the front, back, and sleeves, it is best to assemble as follows:

1) Seam the shoulders of the front and back pieces.
2) Finish the neck edge (the pattern instructions will tell you how to do this).
3) Seam the top of the sleeves to the body of the sweater.
4) Sew continually from the end of the sleeve to the underarm and then down the body of the sweater to the bottom edge.

The sweater map on page 6 shows you how everything fits together and explains what you need to do to prepare each piece.

Note that the sweater map on page 6 shows a sweater with a set-in (shaped) armhole and sleeves with shaped caps. Drop-shoulder sweaters do not have shaped armholes, and the sleeves do not have shaped caps. You will still assemble this type of sweater as described here, but the armhole edges and top of the sleeves will be straight.

Sweater Map

Sweaters vary in silhouette, neckline, assembly, and many other ways. It may be helpful to first read the entire pattern before beginning to knit so you have an idea of what to expect as you work.

Back armhole: Bind off stitches at beginning of right-side rows; work single decrease at beginning of right-side rows.

Sleeve cap: Ease the cap into the front and back armholes when putting together.

Back neck: Bind off center stitches.

Back armhole: Bind off stitches at beginning of wrong-side rows; work single decrease at end of right-side rows.

Shoulders: Seam the front and back shoulders together either by sewing the bound-off stitches together, or use the Three-Needle Bind-off.

Sleeves: (make both sleeves exactly alike)

Right front armhole: Bind off stitches at beginning of wrong-side rows; work single decrease at end of right-side rows.

Front neck: Bind off center stitches.

Left front armhole: Bind off stitches at beginning of right-side rows; work single decrease at beginning of right-side rows.

Ribbing: Usually worked with smaller size needles.

SEAMING

To join the pieces together, you will need a tapestry needle and yarn. Line up the pieces by finding the cast-on stitches on both sides, and then place pins to hold them together. Next, count up about 10 rows on each side and pin the corresponding stitches together. Keep at it until you reach the tops of the two pieces. You may have to ease in extra rows if one piece is slightly longer than the other. Once you have everything pinned, seam using one of the following methods appropriate for each particular seam

How to Begin Seaming

If you have a long tail left from your cast-on row, you can use this strand to begin sewing. To make a neat join at the lower edge with no gap, use the technique shown here.

Thread the strand into a yarn needle. With the right sides of both pieces facing you, insert the yarn needle from back to front into the corner stitch of the piece without the tail. Making a figure eight with the yarn, insert the needle from back to front into the stitch with the cast-on tail. Tighten to close the gap.

Vertical Seam on Stockinette Stitch

The vertical seam is worked from the right side and is used to join two edges row by row. It hides the uneven stitches at the edge of a row and creates an invisible seam, so the knitting appears continuous.

Insert the yarn needle under the horizontal bar between the first and second stitches. Insert the needle into the corresponding bar on the other piece. Continue alternating from side to side.

Vertical Seam on Garter Stitch

This seam joins two edges row by row, like vertical seaming on stockinette stitch. The alternating pattern of catching top and bottom loops of the stitches ensures that only you can tell there's a join.

Insert the yarn needle into the top loop on one side, then in the bottom loop of the corresponding stitch on the other side. Continue to alternate in this way.

Vertical Seam on Ribbing

Knit to knit

When joining ribbing with a knit stitch at each edge, insert the yarn needle under the horizontal bar in the center of a knit stitch on each side in order to keep the pattern continuous.

Purl to purl

When joining ribbing with a purl stitch at each edge, use the bottom loop of the purl stitch on one side and the top loop of the corresponding purl stitch on the other side.

Horizontal Seam on Stockinette Stitch

This seam is used to join two bound-off edges, as for shoulder seams or hoods, and is worked stitch by stitch. Each piece must have the same number of stitches so that the finished seam will resemble a continuous row of knit stitches. Be sure to pull the yarn tightly enough to hide the bound-off edges.

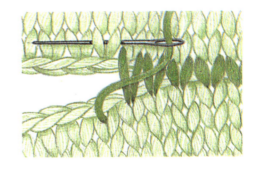

With the bound-off edges together, and lined up stitch for stitch, insert the yarn needle under a stitch inside the bound-off edge of one side and then under the corresponding stitch on the other side. Repeat all the way across the join.

Vertical to Horizontal Seam

Used to connect a bound-off edge to a vertical length of knitted fabric, this seam requires careful pre-measuring and marking to ensure an even seam.

Insert the yarn needle under a stitch inside the bound-off edge of the vertical piece. Insert the needle under one or two horizontal bars between the first and second stitches of the horizontal piece (opposite on stockinette stitch).

Slip-Stitch Crochet Seam
This method creates a visible, though very strong, seam Use it when you don't mind a bulky join or are looking for an especially sturdy connection

With the right sides held together, insert the crochet hook through both thicknesses. Catch the yarn and draw a loop through. *Insert the hook again. Draw a loop through both thicknesses and the loop on the hook. Repeat from *, keeping the stitches straight and even.

Backstitch
The backstitch creates a strong, neat, bulky seam that's perfect for extra reinforcement. With the right sides of the pieces facing each other, secure the seam by taking the needle twice around the edges from back to front.

Bring the needle up about ¼"/5mm from where the yarn last emerged, as shown. In one motion, insert the needle into the point where the yarn emerged from the previous stitch and back up approximately ¼"/5mm ahead of the emerging yarn. Pull the yarn through. Repeat this step, keeping the stitches straight and even.

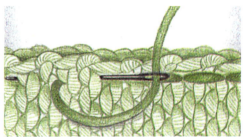

Three-Needle Bind-Off
This is a bind-off that joins two sets of live stitches together to form a seam.
This is often used to join shoulders. Note that each piece must have the same number of stitches.

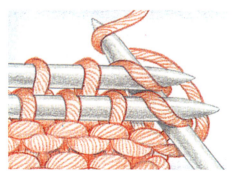  

1) Hold right sides of pieces together on two needles. Insert third needle knitwise into first stitch of each needle, and wrap yarn knitwise.

2) Knit these two stitches together, and slip them off the needles. *Knit the next two stitches together in the same manner.

3) Slip first stitch on third needle over second st and off needle. Rep from * in step 2 across row until all stitches are bound off.

PICKING UP STITCHES

Some sweaters require you to pick up stitches to add a collar, cuff, or ribbing. Picking up stitches simply means that you'll use a needle or crochet hook to dip a new strand of yarn in and out of the edge of your knitted fabric, creating new loops to serve as a foundation row for additional knitting. It's very easy to do, as long as you keep two things in mind: **1.** Make sure you start picking up with the right side facing out, and **2.** Space those new stitches evenly across the fabric.

1) Insert the knitting needle into the corner stitch of the first row, one stitch in from the side edge. Wrap the yarn around the needle knitwise

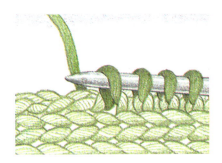

2) Draw yarn through. You have picked up one stitch. Continue to pick up stitches along edge. Occasionally skip one row to keep the edge from flaring.

Whether along a straight or curved edge, pick up stitches evenly so they will not flare or pull in. Place pins, markers, or yarn, every 2"/5cm (see photo at left), and pick up the same number of stitches between each pair of markers. If you know the number of stitches to be picked up, divide this by the number of sections to determine how many stitches to pick up in each one. If you don't have a final count, use the marked sections to ensure even spacing.

Picking Up Along Curved Edge with Knitting Needle

Picking up stitches along a shaped edge
Pick up stitches neatly just inside the shaped edge, following the curve and hiding the jagged selvage.

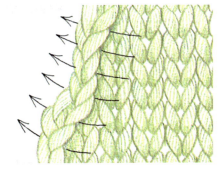

Picking up stitches along a diagonal edge
Pick up stitches one stitch in from the shaped edge, keeping them in a straight line.

Picking Up with Crochet Hook

1) Insert the crochet hook from front to back into the center of the first stitch one row below the bound-off edge. Catch the yarn and pull a loop through.

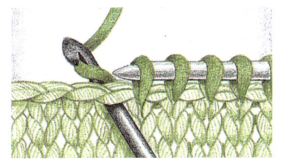

2) Slip the loop onto the knitting needle, being sure it is not twisted. Continue to pick up one stitch in each stitch along the bound-off edge.

Cable-Rib Pullover

Intermediate

SIZES
Small (Medium, Large, X-Large, XX-Large). Shown in size Small.

MEASUREMENTS
Bust 36 (39½, 43, 46, 50)"/91.5 (100, 109, 117, 127)cm*
Length 23¾ (24¼, 24¾, 25¼, 25¾)"/60 (61.5, 63, 64, 65.5)cm
Upper arm 14 (14¾, 15½, 16¾, 17½)"/35.5 (37.5, 39.5, 42.5, 44.5)cm
*Due to the elasticity of the k6, p2 rib, the garment will stretch to fit.

MATERIALS
Yarn
Any worsted-weight wool/acrylic blend, approx 3½oz/100g, 220yd/201m per skein
• 5 (6, 6, 7, 8) skeins in Light Gray

Needles
• One pair size 7 (4.5mm) needles, *or size to obtain gauge*
• One size 7 (4.5mm) circular needle, 16"/40cm long

Notions
• Cable needle (cn)
• Stitch markers

GAUGE
19 sts and 25 rows to 4"/10cm over k6, p2 rib, slightly stretched, using size 7 (4.5mm) needles.
TAKE TIME TO CHECK YOUR GAUGE.

STITCH GLOSSARY
6-St LC Sl 3 sts to cn and hold to front, k3, k3 from cn.

BACK
Cast on 86 (94, 102, 110, 118) sts.
Row 1 (WS) P2, *k2, p2; rep from * to end.
Row 2 K2, *p2, k2; rep from * to end.
Rep rows 1 and 2 for k2, p2 rib for 10 rows.

Begin Rib Pattern
Row 1 (WS) P6, *k2, p6; rep from * to end.
Row 2 K6, *p2, k6; rep from * to end.
Rep last 2 rows for k6, p2 rib, work even for 1 (1, 5, 7, 7) rows more.
Cable row (RS) [K6, p2] 1 (2, 2, 3, 3) times, work 6-st LC in the next k6 rib, work even in rib to end.
Work even in rib for 15 rows.
Shifting cable row (RS) Work in k6, p2 rib until previous k6 rib that was worked as a cable has been worked, then p2, work 6-st LC in the next k6 rib, work even in rib to end.
Rep the last 16 rows until a total of 8 cables have been worked, AT THE SAME TIME, when piece measures approx 15¾"/40cm from beg, work as foll:

Shape Armhole
Bind off 4 (4, 5, 6, 7) sts at beg of next 2 rows, 3 sts at beg of next 2 rows, 2 sts at beg of next 2 rows. Dec 1 st each side of next row then every other row 0 (3, 4, 6, 7) times more—66 (68, 72, 74, 78) sts. Work even until armhole measures 7½ (8, 8½, 9, 9½)"/19 (20.5, 21.5, 23, 24)cm. Pm to mark center 30 sts on last WS row.

Shape Neck and Shoulder
Next row (RS) Bind off 8 (8, 9, 10, 11) sts, work to center marked sts, join a 2nd ball of yarn and bind off center 30 sts, work to end. Working both sides at once, bind off 8 (8, 9, 10, 11) sts at beg of next WS, then 8 (9, 10, 10, 11) sts from each shoulder edge once, AT THE SAME TIME, bind off 2 sts from each neck edge once.

FRONT
Work same as back until armhole measures 5¼ (5¾, 6¼, 6¾, 7¼)"/13.5 (14.5, 16, 17, 18.5)cm.

Shape Neck
Next row (RS) Work 28 (29, 31, 32, 34) sts, join a 2nd ball of yarn and bind off center 10 sts, work to end.
Working both sides at once, bind off 3 sts from each neck edge twice, 2 sts twice, 1 st twice—16 (17, 19, 20, 22) sts rem each side. Work even until armhole measures same as back to shoulder.

Shape Shoulder
Bind off 8 (8, 9, 10, 11) sts from each shoulder

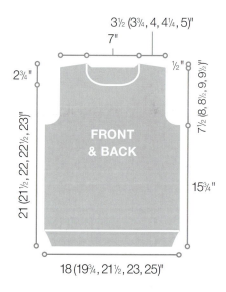

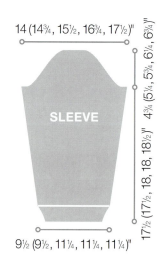

edge once, 8 (9, 10, 10, 11) sts once.

SLEEVES
Cast on 46 (46, 54, 54, 54) sts. Work in k2, p2 rib as on back for 12 rows.

Begin Rib Pattern
Work rows 1 and 2 of k6, p2 rib as on back. Then, cont in k6, p2 rib for 5 rows more.
Inc row (RS) Inc 1 st in rib pat, work to last st, inc 1 st in rib pat. Rep inc row every 6th row 0 (4, 0, 5, 0) times more, every 8th row 9 (7, 9, 7, 9) times more—66 (70, 74, 80, 84) sts.
Work even until piece measures 17½ (17½, 18, 18, 18½)"/44.5 (44.5, 45.5, 45.5, 47)cm from beg.

Shape Cap
Bind off 4 (4, 5, 6, 7) sts at beg of next 2 rows, 3 sts at beg of next 2 rows, 2 sts at beg of next 2 rows. Dec 1 st each side of next row then every other row 9 (11, 12, 14, 15) times more. Bind off 2 sts at beg of next 2 rows, bind off 3 sts at beg of next 2 rows. Bind off rem 18 sts.

FINISHING
Block pieces to measurements. Sew shoulder seams.

Neckband
With RS facing and circular needle, pick up and k 40 sts from back neck edge, 48 sts from front neck edge—88 sts. Join to work in rnds and pm to mark beg of rnds. Work in rnds of k2, p2 rib for 1"/2.5cm. Bind off in rib.

Set in sleeves. Sew side and sleeve seams.•

Design Note
When working the decreases for the neck, shoulders, and sleeve caps, it might be helpful to keep a tally of what you've worked as you progress.

Textured V-Neck Sweater

Intermediate

SIZES
Small (Medium, Large, 1X, 2X). Shown in size Small.

MEASUREMENTS
Bust 36 (40, 44, 48, 52)"/91.5 (101.5, 111.5, 122, 132)cm
Length 22 (22½, 23½, 24, 25)"/56 (57, 59.5, 61, 63.5)cm
Upper arm 14 (15, 16, 17, 18)"/35.5 (38, 40.5, 43, 45.5)cm

MATERIALS
Yarn
Any worsted-weight wool/llama/bamboo/Donegal blend, approx 1¾oz/50g, 109yd/100m per skein
- 14 (16, 18, 20, 22) skeins in Orange

Needles
- One pair size 8 (5mm) needles, *or size to obtain gauge*
- One size 8 (5mm) circular needle, 24"/60cm long

Notions
- Stitch holder
- Removable stitch markers

GAUGE
24 sts and 40 rows to 4"/10cm over garter slip st using size 8 (5mm) needles.
TAKE TIME TO CHECK YOUR GAUGE.

K1, P1 RIB
(multiple of 2 sts plus 1)
Row 1 (RS) K1, *p1, k1; rep from * to end.
Row 2 P1, *k1, p1; rep from * to end.
Rep rows 1 and 2 for k1, p1 rib.

GARTER SLIP STITCH
(multiple of 2 sts plus 1)
Rows 1 and 2 Knit.
Row 3 (RS) K1, *sl 1 purlwise wyib, k1; rep from * to end.
Row 4 K1, *sl 1 purlwise wyif, k1; rep from * to end.
Rep rows 1–4 for garter slip st.

BACK
Cast on 109 (121, 133, 145, 157) sts. Work in k1, p1 rib for 1"/2.5cm, end with a WS row. Work in garter slip st until piece measures 14 (14, 14½, 14½, 15)"/35.5 (35.5, 37, 37, 38)cm from beg, end with a WS row.

Shape Armholes
Bind off 5 (7, 9, 11, 13) sts at beg of next 2 rows. Dec 1 st each side every row 4 (5, 6, 7, 8) times—91 (97, 103, 109, 115) sts. Work even until armhole measures 7½ (8, 8½, 9, 9½)"/19 (20.5, 21.5, 23, 24)cm, end with a WS row.

Shape Shoulders and Neck
Bind off 9 (10, 10, 11, 12) sts at beg of next 2 rows, 8 (9, 10, 11, 12) sts at beg of next 2 rows, then 8 (9, 10, 11, 11) sts at beg of next 2 rows. AT THE SAME TIME, bind off center 21 (21, 23, 23, 25) sts, then bind off 5 sts from each neck edge twice.

FRONT
Work as for back until armhole measures 1½"/4cm, end with a WS row. Cont to shape armholes, if necessary, AT THE SAME TIME, work as foll:

Shape V-Neck
Next row (RS) Work to center st, place center st on holder, join a 2nd ball of yarn, work to end. Working both sides at once, work next row even. Dec 1 st from each neck edge on next row, then every other row 19 (19, 20, 20, 21) times more—25 (28, 30, 33, 35) sts each side. Work even until piece measures same as back to shoulder, end with a WS row.
Shape shoulders as for back.

SLEEVES
Cast on 57 (57, 59, 59, 61) sts. Work in k1, p1 rib for 1"/2.5cm, end with a WS row. Work in garter slip st for 1"/2.5cm, end with a WS row.
Inc 1 st each side on next row, then every 10th (8th, 8th, 6th, 6th) row 2 (5, 13, 7, 13) times more, then every 12th (10th, 10th, 8th, 8th) row 10 (10, 4, 13, 9) times—83 (89, 95, 101, 107) sts.
Work even until piece measures 17 (17,

Design Note
Because V-necks extend further down the front of a sweater, you will begin the neckline shaping much earlier and carry it through to the end of the piece.

17½, 17½, 18)"/43 (43, 44.5, 44.5, 45.5)cm from beg, end with a WS row.

Shape Cap
Bind off 5 (7, 9, 11, 13) sts at beg of next 2 rows. Dec 1 st each side every row 4 (6, 6, 8, 8), every other row 11 (12, 16, 20, 22) times, then every row 12 (10, 7, 2, 2) times—19 (19, 19, 19, 17) sts. Bind off knitwise.

FINISHING
Block pieces to measurements. Sew shoulder seams.

Neckband
With RS facing and circular needle, beg at left shoulder seam and pick up and k 42 (44, 46, 48, 50) sts evenly spaced along left neck edge, k1 from holder for center st, pm on center st, pick up and k 42 (44, 46, 48, 50) sts evenly spaced along right neck edge to right shoulder, pick up and k 37 (37, 39, 39, 41) sts evenly spaced across back neck—122 (126, 132, 136, 142) sts. Join and pm for beg of rnd.
Set-up rnd *K1, p1; rep from * to last st, p1.
Next rnd Work in rib to 1 st before center st, S2KP, work in rib to end.
Rep last rnd 5 times more. Bind off all sts loosely in rib.

Set in sleeves. Sew side and sleeve seams.
Weave in ends.•

Raglan Turtleneck Sweater

Intermediate

SIZES
Small (Medium, Large, X-Large, XX-Large, 1X). Shown in size Small.

MEASUREMENTS
Bust 38 (40, 42½, 45, 47, 50½)"/96.5 (101.5, 108, 114, 119, 128)cm
Length 26 (26, 26¼, 26¼, 27, 27½)"/66 (66, 66.5, 66.5, 68.5, 70)cm
Upper arm 13½ (14½, 15½, 17, 18, 19)"/34 (37, 39.5, 43, 45.5, 48)cm

MATERIALS
Yarn
Any worsted-weight wool, approx 1¾oz/50g, 122yd/112m per skein
• 9 (10, 11, 12, 13, 14) skeins in Green-Blue

Needles
• One pair each sizes 5 and 7 (3.75 and 4.5mm) needles, *or size to obtain gauge*
• One each sizes 5 and 7 (3.75 and 4.5mm) circular needle, each 16"/40cm long

Notions
• Stitch markers
• Stitch holder

GAUGE
20 sts and 28 rows to 4"/10cm over St st using larger needles.
TAKE TIME TO CHECK YOUR GAUGE.

NOTE
One selvage st worked on each end of every row does not figure into the finished measurements.

BACK
With smaller needles, cast on 118 (126, 134, 142, 150, 158) sts.
Row 1 (RS) *K2, p2; rep from * to last 2 sts, k2.
Row 2 *P2, k2; rep from * to last 2 sts, p2.
Rep rows 1 and 2 until piece measures 3"/7.5cm from beg.
Dec row (RS) K5 (5, 3, 3, 1, 5), [k2tog, k3] 21 (23, 25, 27, 29, 29) times, k2tog, k6 (4, 4, 2, 2, 6)—96 (102, 108, 114, 120, 128) sts.
Change to larger needles.
Beg with a purl (WS) row, work in St st (k on RS, p on WS) until piece measures 17½ (17, 16½, 16, 16, 16)"/44.5 (43, 42, 40.5, 40.5, 40.5)cm from beg.

Shape Raglan Armhole
Bind off 2 (2, 3, 4, 5, 5) sts at beg of next 2 rows—92 (98, 102, 106, 110, 118) sts.
Row 1 (RS) K3, p1, k to last 4 sts, p1, k3.
Row 2 (WS) P3, k1, p to last 4 sts, k1, p3.
Dec row 3 (RS) K3, p1, ssk, k to last 6 sts, k2tog, p1, k3—2 sts dec'd.
Rep last 2 rows 22 (24, 26, 28, 30, 32) times more—46 (48, 48, 48, 48, 52) sts.
Next row Rep row 2.
Next row Rep row 1.
Next row Rep row 2.
Next row Rep dec row 3.
Rep last 4 rows twice more—40 (42, 42, 42, 42, 46) sts.
Next row Rep row 2.
Bind off.

FRONT
Work as for back, including the raglan armhole shaping, until there are 50 (52, 52, 52, 52, 56) sts. On the last WS row, pm to mark center 16 (18, 18, 18, 18, 22) sts.

Shape Neck
Cont to work raglan armhole shaping every other row twice more, then every 4th row 3 times, AT THE SAME TIME, work the neck shaping as foll:
Next row (RS) K3, p1, ssk, k to marked sts, sl center 16 (18, 18, 18, 18, 22) sts to holder, join 2nd ball of yarn and k to last 6 sts, k2tog, p1, k3.
Working both sides at once, bind off 3 sts from each neck edge once, 2 sts once, then dec 1 st each side every other row 5 times. After all shaping is completed, k2tog on rem sts each side and fasten off.

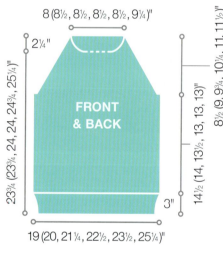

SLEEVES

With smaller needles, cast on 42 (46, 50, 58, 62, 66) sts.

Work in k2, p2 rib as on back for 3"/7.5cm, dec 2 (2, 0, 2, 0, 0) sts on the last WS row—40 (44, 50, 56, 62, 66) sts. Change to larger needles. Work in St st for 6 rows.
Inc row (RS) K1, kfb, k to last 3 sts, kfb, k2—2 sts inc'd.
Rep inc row (every alternate 8th and 6th row) a total of 14 times more—70 (74, 80, 86, 92, 96) sts. Work even until piece measures 19"/48cm from beg.

Shape Raglan Cap
Work same as the back raglan armhole shaping. Place rem 14 sts on a st holder.

FINISHING
Block pieces to measurements. Sew raglan sleeve caps into raglan armholes. Sew side and sleeve seams.

Turtleneck
From the RS using smaller circular needle, pick up and k 40 (42, 42, 42, 42, 46) sts from back neck, 14 sts from sleeve holder, pick up and k 16 sts from shaped front neck edge k 16 (18, 18, 18, 18, 22) sts from front neck holder, pick up and k 16 sts from shaped front neck edge, k14 sts from sleeve holder—116 (120, 120, 120, 120, 128) sts. Join to work in rnds and pm to mark beg of rnds. Work in rnds of k2, p2 rib for 4"/10cm.
Change to larger circular needle and cont in k2, p2 rib until turtleneck measures 10"/25.5cm. Bind off loosely in rib. •

Design Note
Small details can make a big difference. This raglan sweater has simple textures added along the shoulder decreases.

Honeycomb Sweater

Intermediate

SIZES
Small (Medium, Large, X-Large, XX-Large). Shown in size Medium.

MEASUREMENTS
Bust 36 (38, 40, 42, 44)"/91.5 (96.5, 101.5, 106.5, 111.5)cm
Length 23 (23½, 24, 24½, 25)"/58.5 (59.5, 61, 62, 63.5)cm
Upper arm 12½ (13½, 14½, 15½, 16½)"/31.5 (34, 37, 39.5, 42)cm

MATERIALS
Yarn 4
Any worsted-weight wool/silk blend, approx 3½oz/100g, 200yd/199m per skein
- 5 (5, 6, 6, 7) skeins in Purple

Needles
- One pair size 8 (5mm) needles, *or size to obtain gauge*
- One size 8 (5mm) circular needle, 29"/74cm long
- One set (5) size 8 (5mm) double-pointed needles (dpn)

Notions
- Stitch holder
- Stitch markers
- Scrap yarn

GAUGE
17 sts and 25 rows/rnds to 4"/10cm over St st using size 8 (5mm) needles.
TAKE TIME TO CHECK YOUR GAUGE.

HONEYCOMB PATTERN (worked in rows)
(over an odd number of sts)
Row 1 (RS) Knit.
Row 2 K1, *sl 1 wyib, k1; rep from * to end.
Row 3 Knit.
Row 4 K2, *sl 1 wyib, k1; rep from * to last st, k1.
Rep rows 1–4 for honeycomb pat.

HONEYCOMB PATTERN (worked in rnds)
(over an even number of sts in rounds)
Rnd 1 Knit.
Rnd 2 *P1, sl 1 wyif; rep from * around.
Rnd 3 Knit.
Rnd 4 *Sl 1 wyif, p1; rep from * around.
Rep rnds 1–4 for honeycomb pat.

NOTE
Pullover is worked by beg at the shoulder edge then back and front are worked separately to the armhole. Then, pieces are joined to work in rounds for the body and the sleeves are picked up along the armhole edges and worked to the cuffs.

BACK
Right Back Shoulder
Cast on 23 (25, 27, 29, 31) sts. Work in honeycomb pat in rows for 4 rows. Sl sts to a st holder.

Left Back Shoulder
Work as for right back shoulder for 4 rows.

Join Shoulders
Joining row (RS) K the 23 (25, 27, 29, 31) sts of left back shoulder, then turn and cast on 31 sts for the neck, then from the RS, k the 23 (25, 27, 29, 31) sts of right back shoulder—77 (81, 85, 89, 93) sts. Working on all back sts, work even until piece measures 6 (6½, 7, 7½, 8)"/15 (16.5, 18, 19, 20.5)cm.
Sl sts to scrap yarn.

FRONT
Front Left Shoulder
With RS facing, pick up and k 23 (25, 27, 29, 31) sts along cast-on edge of back left shoulder and beg with WS row 2, work in honeycomb pat st in rows for 10 rows. Sl sts to a holder.

Right Front Shoulder
With RS facing, pick up and k 23 (25, 27, 29, 31) sts along cast-on edge of back right shoulder and beg with WS row 2, work in honeycomb pat st in rows for 10 rows.

Join Shoulders
Joining row (RS) K the 23 (25, 27, 29, 31) sts of front right shoulder, turn and cast on 31 sts for the neck, then from the RS, k the 23 (25, 27, 29, 31) sts of front left shoulder—77 (81, 85, 89, 93) sts.
Work even until piece measures same as back with the same number of rows from the shoulder.

BODY
Rnd 1 (RS) K the back sts then k the front sts—154 (162, 170, 178, 186) sts.
Join to work in rnds and pm to mark beg of rnd. Cont in St st (k every rnd) for 3"/7.5cm.
Set-up rnd K26 (27, 28, 30, 31), pm, k26 (27, 28, 29, 31), pm, k51 (54, 57, 60, 62), pm, k26 (27, 28, 29, 31), pm, k25 (27, 29, 30, 31).
Dec rnd *K to 2 sts before marker, ssk, sm, k to next marker, sm, k2tog; rep from * once more, k to end—4 sts dec'd.
Rep dec rnd every 10th row 3 times more—138 (146, 154, 162, 170) sts.
Work even until body measures 9"/23cm from the underarm.
Inc rnd *K to 1 st before marker, kfb, sm, k to next marker, sm, kfb; rep from * once more, k to end—4 sts inc'd.
Rep inc rnd every 6th rnd 3 times more—154 (162, 170, 178, 186) sts.
Work even until body measures 15½"/39.5cm.
Work in honeycomb pat st in rnds for 16 rnds. Bind off.

SLEEVES
With dpn and RS facing, pick up and k 54

Design Note
There are many ways to knit a sweater, and this one is worked from the top down by knitting each shoulder separately before joining to work in the round. Try it out!

Honeycomb Sweater

(58, 62, 66, 70) sts around armhole edge. Divide sts over 4 dpn with 13 (14, 15, 16, 17) sts on needles 1 and 3 and 14 (15, 16, 17, 18) sts on needles 2 and 4.
Join and pm to mark beg of rnd. Work in rnds of St st for 2¼"/6cm.
Dec rnd K1, k2tog, k to the last 3 sts, ssk, k1.
Rep dec rnd every 7th rnd 12 (12, 12, 13, 13) times more—28 (32, 36, 38, 42) sts.
Work even until sleeve measures 18"/45.5cm.
Work in honeycomb pat st in rnds for 16 rnds. Bind off.

FINISHING
Weave in ends. Block to measurments.•

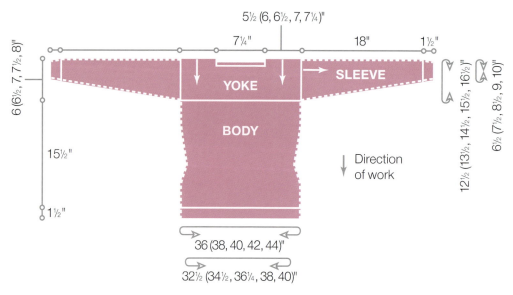

Striped Boat-Neck Sweater

Intermediate

SIZES
Small (Medium, Large, X-Large, 1X, 2X). Shown in size Medium.

MEASUREMENTS
Bust 36 (38, 40, 42½, 45, 48)"/91.5 (96.5, 101.5, 108, 114, 122)cm
Length 25 (25½, 26, 26½, 27, 27½)"/ 63.5 (64.5, 66, 67.5, 68.5, 70)cm
Upper arm 13¼ (13½, 14½, 15, 16, 17)"/33.5 (34, 37, 38, 40.5, 43)cm

MATERIALS
Yarn
Any worsted-weight cotton, approx 3½oz/100g, 205yd/187m per skein
- 3 (3, 4, 4, 4, 5) skeins in White (A)
- 2 (2, 2, 3, 3, 3) skeins in Yellow (B)

Needles
- One pair each sizes 6 and 7 (4 and 4.5mm) needles, *or size to obtain gauge*
- One size 6 (4mm) circular needle, 24"/100cm long

Notions
- One size E/4 (3.5mm) crochet hook
- One ¾"/20mm button

GAUGE
20 sts and 25 rows to 4"/10cm over St st using larger needles.
TAKE TIME TO CHECK YOUR GAUGE.

STRIPE PATTERN
Working in St st (k on RS, p on WS), beg with a purl row, work *4 rows A, 2 rows B; rep from * (6 rows) for stripe pat.

BACK
With smaller needles and A, using long-tail cast-on, cast on 90 (94, 100, 106, 112, 120) sts. [K 1 row, p 1 row] twice.
Hem joining row (RS) With the 4-row hem folded up to meet the working sts on the needle, using RH needle, *k 1 matching st from the cast-on edge simultaneously with the st on the needle; rep from * until all sts are joined from the hem.** Change to larger needles.

Striped Boat-Neck Sweater

Begin Stripe Pattern
Using A and beg with a purl row, work in stripe pat for 7 rows.
Dec row (RS) K2, k2tog, k to last 4 sts, SKP, k2.
Rep dec row every 8th row 4 times more—80 (84, 90, 96, 102, 110) sts.
Work even in stripe pat until piece measures 11"/28cm from beg.
Inc row (RS) K2, kfb, k to last 4 sts, kfb, k3.
Rep inc row every 6th row 4 times more—90 (94, 110, 106, 112, 120) sts.
Work even until piece measures approx 17"/43cm from beg, ending with row 5 (in B) of the 17th stripe rep.

Shape Armhole
Bind off 5 (5, 5, 5, 6, 6) sts at beg of next 2 rows, 2 sts at beg of next 2 rows.
Dec row 1 (RS) K to last 4 sts, SKP, k2.
Dec row 2 (RS) P to last 4 sts, p2tog, k2.
Rep dec rows 1 and 2 for 1 (2, 3, 5, 5, 7) times more—72 (74, 78, 80, 84, 88) sts.
Cont in stripe pat as established until there are 19 reps of the stripe pat from beg. Discontinue stripe pat and cont to work with A only to end of piece, AND, work even until armhole measures 2½ (2½, 3, 3, 3½, 4)"/6.5 (6.5, 7.5, 7.5, 9, 10)cm.

Separate for Back Opening
Next row (RS) K 33 (34, 36, 37, 39, 41), p1, k2, join 2nd ball of A and k2, p1, k to end.
Next row P to last 3 sts on first side, k1, p2; on 2nd side, p2, k1, p to end.
Cont as established, working both sides at once with separate balls of yarn, until armhole measures 6½ (7, 7½, 8, 8½, 9)"/16.5 (18, 19, 20.5, 21.5, 23)cm.

Shape Neck
Bind off 18 sts from each neck edge once, 5 sts once, 3 sts twice, AT THE SAME TIME, when armhole measures 7 (7½, 8, 8½, 9, 9½)"/17.5 (19, 20.5, 21.5, 23, 24)cm, bind off 2 (3, 3, 4, 4, 5) sts from each shoulder edge twice, 3 (2, 4, 3, 5, 5) sts once.

FRONT

Work as for back, only without the back opening, until armhole measures 5 (5½, 6, 6½, 7, 7½)"/12.5 (14, 15, 16.5, 18, 19)cm.

Shape Neck
Next row (RS) K 26 (27, 29, 30, 32, 34) sts, join 2nd ball of yarn and bind off center 20 sts, k to end.
Cont to shape neck, binding off 5 sts from each neck edge twice, then 3 sts 3 times—7 (8, 10, 11, 13, 15) sts rem each side.
Work even until armhole measures 7 (7½, 8, 8½, 9, 9½)"/17.5 (19, 20.5, 21.5, 23, 24)cm.

Shape shoulder
Bind off 2 (3, 3, 4, 4, 5) sts from each shoulder edge twice, 3 (2, 4, 3, 5, 5) sts once.

SLEEVES

With smaller needles and A, cast on 56 (58, 62, 64, 70, 74) sts. Work hem joining up to the ** as on back. Change to larger needles. Then work in stripe pat for 9 rows.
Inc row (RS) K2, kfb, k to last 4 sts, kfb, k3.
Rep inc row every 10th row 4 times more—66 (68, 72, 74, 80, 84) sts.
Work even until piece measures approx 12"/30.5cm from beg, ending with row 5 (in B) of the 12th stripe rep.

Shape Cap
Bind off 5 (5, 5, 5, 6, 7) sts at beg of next 2 rows, 2 sts at beg of next 2 rows—52 (54, 58, 60, 64, 66) sts.

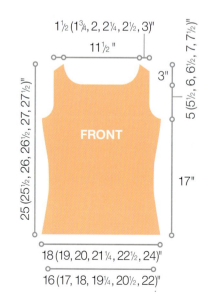

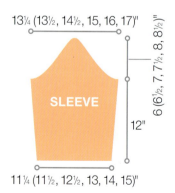

Dec row 1 (RS) K to last 4 sts, SKP, k2.
Dec row 2 (WS) P to last 4 sts, p2tog, k2.
Rep dec rows 1 and 2 for 12 (13, 15, 16, 18, 19) times more—26 sts.
Dec row 3 (RS) K to last 5 sts, SK2P, k2.
Dec row 4 (WS) P to last 5 sts, p3tog, k2.
Rep dec rows 1 and 2 for 3 times more. Bind off rem 10 sts.

FINISHING
Block finished pieces to measurements. Sew shoulder seams.

Neckband
With RS facing, size 6 (4mm) circular needle, and A, leaving a long end, pick up and k 122 sts evenly around neck edge. [P 1 row, k 1 row] twice. Bind off. Turn neckband to the RS and tack in place.
Using crochet hook and ½ (split) strand from the long end, ch 7 tightly and join to form a button loop. Sew on button.
Weave in ends. Block finished piece lightly.

Set in sleeves. Sew side and sleeve seams.•

Design Note
Who says sweaters are only for winter? This sweater, knit in cotton, is a great warm weather top, complete with a playful peekaboo opening on the back

Twists and Cables Sweater

Intermediate

SIZES
X-Small (Small, Medium, Large).
Shown in size X-Small.

MEASUREMENTS
Bust 31 (34, 37, 40)"/78.5 (86.5, 94, 101.5)cm
Length 24¾ (24¾, 25¾, 27¼)"/63 (63, 65.5, 69)cm
Upper arm 12 (12, 14, 15½)"/30.5 (30.5, 35.5, 39.5)cm

MATERIALS
Yarn 5
Any bulky-weight alpaca, approx 3½oz/100g, 110yd/101m per skein
• 5 (6, 6, 7) skeins in Beige (A)
• 4 (5, 6, 6) skeins in Coral (B)

Needles
• One pair each sizes 10 and 11 (6 and 8mm) needles, *or size to obtain gauges*
• One size 9 (5.5mm) circular needle, 24"/60cm long

Notions
• Cable needle (cn)
• Stitch holders
• Stitch markers

GAUGES
• 13 sts and 16 rows to 4"/10cm over twisted St st using size 11 (8mm) needles.
• 16 sts and 16 rows to 4"/10cm over lattice cable pat using size 11 (8mm) needles.
TAKE TIME TO CHECK YOUR GAUGES.

SHORT ROW WRAP & TURN (w&t)
on RS row (on WS row)
1) Wyib (wyif), sl next st purlwise.
2) Move yarn between the needles to the front (back).
3) Sl the same st back to LH needle. Turn work. One st is wrapped.
4) When working the wrapped st, insert RH needle under the wrap and work it tog with the corresponding st on needle.

STITCH GLOSSARY
4-st LC Sl 2 sts to cn and hold to front, k2, k2 from cn.
6-st LC Sl 3 sts to cn and hold to front, k3, k3 from cn.
6-st RC Sl 3 sts to cn and hold to back, k3, k3 from cn.
6-st dec LC Sl 3 sts to cn and hold to front, k1, k2tog, k3 from cn—1 st dec'd.
6-st dec RC Sl 3 sts to cn and hold to back, k1, k2tog, k3 from cn—1 st dec'd.

TWISTED STOCKINETTE STITCH
(over any number of sts)
Row 1 (RS) *K1 tbl; rep from * to end.
Row 2 Purl.
Rep rows 1 and 2 for twisted St st.

LATTICE CABLE PATTERN
(multiple of 6 sts plus 2)
Row 1 (RS) Knit.
Rows 2, 4, and 6 Purl.
Row 3 (RS) K1, *6-st LC; rep from *, end k1.
Row 5 Knit.
Row 7 (RS) K4, *6-st RC; rep from *, end k4.
Row 8 Purl.
Rep rows 1–8 for lattice cable pat.

NOTE
Make front first.

FRONT
With size 10 (6mm) needles and A, cast on 52 (56, 60, 64) sts.
Row 1 (RS) P1, *k2, p2; rep from * to last 3 sts, k2, p1.
Cont in k2, p2 rib as established for 9 rows more, inc 0 (1, 2, 3) sts evenly across last WS row—52 (57, 62, 67) sts.
Change to size 11 (8mm) needles and cont in twisted St st until piece measures 14 (14, 14, 14½)"/35.5 (35.5, 35.5, 37)cm from beg, end with a WS row. Cut A and work to end with B only.

Begin Yoke
Row 1 (RS) With B, k1 tbl in each st across.
Row 2 Purl.
Inc cable row 3 (RS) K1, [sl 3 sts to cn and hold to front, k1, kfb, k3 sts from cn] 10 (11, 12, 13) times, k1—62 (68, 74, 80) sts.
Beg with row 4, work in lattice cable pat through row 8, then work rows 1–3. Piece measures approx 16¾ (16¾, 16¾, 17¼)"/42 (42, 42, 43)cm from beg.

Shape Armholes
Row 1 (WS) Bind off 3 sts, p to end.
Row 2 (RS) Bind off 3 sts, k to end.
Row 3 Bind off 2 sts, p to end.
Row 4 Bind off 2 sts, k until 5 sts are on RH needle, [6-st RC] 7 (8, 9, 10) times, k5.
Row 5 Purl.
Row 6 K1, SKP, k to last 3 sts, SKP, k1—50 (56, 62, 68) sts.
Beg with row 2, cont in lattice cable pat until armhole measures approx 6 (6, 7, 8)"/15 (15, 18, 20.5)cm, end with pat row 2 or 6. Place markers to mark center 22 (24, 26, 28) sts on the last WS row.

Shape Neck and Shoulders
Row 1 (RS) Work 14 (16, 18, 20) sts in cable pat as established, work next 22 (24, 26, 28) sts in pat and sl to a st holder for front neck, work to end. Working both sides at once, bind off 3 sts from each neck edge once—11 (13, 15, 17) sts rem each side.

Right Shoulder
Note Shoulders are shaped with short

Twists and Cables Sweater

rows. Final row is worked with dec cables, see stitch glossary.
Row 1 (WS) Work 11 (13, 15, 17) sts.
Short-row 2 (RS) Work in pat to last 5 sts, w&t.
Row 3 Sl 1, p to end.
Short-row 4 K to last 7 (9, 9, 11) sts, w&t.
Row 5 Sl 1, p to end.
Row 6 (RS) Work 11 (13, 15, 17) sts in pat, working 6-st dec LC or RC—10 (11, 13, 15) sts.
Place on a st holder for right shoulder.

Left Shoulder
Join B to 11 (13, 15, 17) left shoulder sts ready to work a WS row.
Short-row 1 (WS) P to last 5 sts, w&t.
Row 2 (RS) Work in pat.
Short-row 3 P to the last 7 (9, 9, 11) sts, w&t.
Row 4 (RS) Sl 1, k to end.
Row 5 Sl 1, p to end.
Row 6 (RS) Work 11 (13, 15, 17) sts in pat, working 6-st dec LC or RC—10 (11, 13, 15) sts.
Place on a st holder for left shoulder.

BACK
Work as for front, omitting neck shaping, until armhole measures same as back to shoulder, end with pat row 2 or 6.

Shape Shoulders
Work shoulder shaping as for back on 11 (13, 15, 17) sts each side. Place center 28 (30, 32, 34) sts on hold for back neck.

SLEEVES
With size 10 (6mm) needles and A, cast on 30 (30, 34, 34) sts.
Row 1 (RS) K1, *k2, p2; rep from * to last st, k1.
Cont in k2, p2 rib as established for 3"/7.5cm, inc 2 (2, 3, 4) sts evenly on the last WS row—32 (32, 37, 38) sts.
Change to size 11 (8mm) needles and cont in twisted St st, inc 1 st each side every 8th (8th, 8th, 6th) row 5 (5, 5, 7) times—42 (42, 47, 52) sts.
Work even until piece measures 14¼"/36cm from beg, end with a WS row. Cut A and work to end with B only.

Begin Lattice Cable Pattern
Row 1 (RS) With B, k1 tbl in each st across.
Row 2 Purl.
Inc cable row 3 (RS) K1, [sl 3 sts to cn and hold to front, k1, kfb, then k3 from cn] 8 (8, 9, 10) times, k1—50 (50, 56, 62) sts.
Beg with row 4, work in lattice cable pat through row 8, then work rows 1–3. Piece measures 17"/43cm from beg.

Shape Cap
Row 1 (WS) Bind off 3 sts, p to end.
Row 2 Bind off 3 sts, k to end.
Row 3 Bind off 2 sts, k to end.
Row 4 Bind off 2 sts, k until 5 sts are on RH needle, [6-st RC] 5 (5, 6, 7) times, k5.
Row 5 Purl.
Row 6 K1, SKP, k to the last 3 sts, k2tog, k1—38 (38, 44, 50) sts.
Row 7 Purl.
Row 8 K1, 6-st dec LC, [6-st LC] 4 (4, 5, 6) times, 6-st dec LC, k1—36 (36, 42, 48) sts.
Row 9 Purl.
Row 10 K1, SK2P, k to last 4 sts, k3tog, k1—32 (32, 38, 44) sts.
Row 11 Purl.
Row 12 K1, 6-st dec RC, [6-st RC] 3 (3, 4, 5) times, 6-st dec RC, k1—30 (30, 36, 42) sts.
Row 13 Purl.
Row 14 Rep row 10—26 (26, 32, 38) sts.
Row 15 Purl.
Row 16 K1, 6-st dec LC, [6-st LC] 2 (2, 3, 4) times, 6-st dec LC, k1—24 (24, 30, 36) sts.
Row 17 Purl.
Row 18 Rep row 10—20 (20, 26, 32) sts.
Row 19 Purl.
Row 20 K1, [sl 3 sts to cn and hold to back, k1, k2tog, then k1, k2tog from cn] 3 (3, 4, 5) times, k1—14 (14, 18, 22) sts.
Work 1 (1, 5, 6) rows even in cable pat on the last 14 (14, 18, 22) sts, working 4-st LC instead of 6-st LC on next row 3 of pat.
Bind off.

FINISHING
Using 3-needle bind-off (see page 8), join shoulders. Set in sleeves. Sew side and sleeve seams.

TURTLENECK
With RS facing, circular needle, and B, k28 (30, 32, 34) sts from back neck holder, then pick up and k 14 sts along shaped front neck edge, k22 (24, 26, 28) sts from front neck holder, pick up and k 14 (13, 15, 14) sts from shaped front neck—78 (81, 87, 90) sts. Join and pm for beg of rnd.
Rnd 1 [Kfb, p2] 26 (27, 29, 30) times—104 (108, 116, 120) sts.
Rnd 2 *K2, p2; rep from * around.
Rep rnd 2 for k2, p2 rib until neck measures 6½"/16.5cm.
Bind off in rib. •

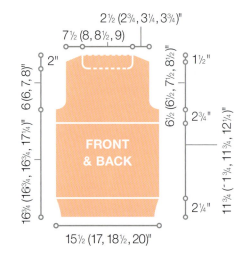

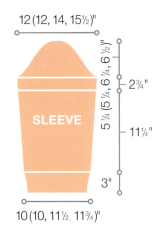

Off-Center Cable Sweater

Easy

SIZES
Small (Medium, Large, X-Large, 2X). Shown in size Small.

MEASUREMENTS
Bust 33 (37, 41, 45, 49)"/84 (94, 104, 114.5, 124.5)cm
Length 21 (21½, 22, 22½, 23)"/53.5 (54.5, 56, 57, 58.5)cm
Upper arm 12 (13, 14, 15, 16)"/30.5 (33, 35.5, 38, 40.5)cm

MATERIALS
Yarn
Any worsted-weight wool, approx 4oz/113g, 225yd/206m per skein
• 4 (5, 5, 5, 6) skeins in Pink

Needles
• One pair size 7 (4.5mm) needles, *or size to obtain gauge*
• One size 5 (3.75mm) circular needle, 16"/40cm long

Notions
• Cable needle (cn)
• Stitch markers
• Stitch holders

GAUGE
20 sts and 27 rows to 4"/10cm over St st using size 7 (4.5mm) needles.
TAKE TIME TO CHECK YOUR GAUGE.

STITCH GLOSSARY
6-st LC Slip 3 sts to cn and hold to front, k3, k3 from cn.
6-st RC Slip 3 sts to cn and hold to back, k3, k3 from cn.

RIB (worked in rows)
(multiple of 5 sts plus 3)
Row 1 (WS) P3, *k2, p3; rep from * to end.
Row 2 K the knit sts and p the purl sts.
Rep row 2 for rib.

RIB (worked in rnds)
(multiple of 5 sts)
Rnd 1 (RS) *K3, p2; rep from * to end.
Rep rnd 1 for rib.

BACK
With size 7 (4.5mm) needles, cast on 83 (93, 103, 113, 123) sts. Work in rib for

Off-Center Cable Sweater

4"/10cm, end with a RS row.
Set-up row (WS) P13 (18, 23, 28, 33), pm, k2, p4, M1, p4, k2, pm, p to end—84 (94, 104, 114, 124) sts.

Begin Chart
Row 1 (RS) K58 (63, 68, 73, 78), sm, work row 1 of chart over next 13 sts, sm, k to end.
Row 2 (WS) P13 (18, 23, 28, 33), sm, work row 2 of chart over 13 sts, p to end.
Cont in this way until piece measures 6"/15cm from beg, end with a WS row.
Dec row (RS) K2, ssk, cont in pat to last 4 sts, k2tog, k2.
Rep dec row every 4th row twice more—78 (88, 98, 108, 118) sts.
Work even in pat until piece measures 8½"/21.5cm from beg, end with a WS row.
Inc row (RS) K2, M1, work to last 2 sts, M1, k2.
Rep inc row every 4th row 3 times more—86 (96, 106, 116, 126) sts.
Work even in pat until piece measures 15"/38cm from beg, end with a WS row.

Shape Armhole
Bind off 5 sts at beg of next 2 rows. Dec 1 st each side every other row 5 times—66 (76, 86, 96, 106) sts.
Work even in pat until armhole measures 6 (6½, 7, 7½, 8)"/15 (16.5, 18, 19, 20.5)cm, end with a WS row. Bind off.

FRONT
With size 7 (4.5mm) needles, cast on 83 (93, 103, 113, 123) sts. Work in rib for 4"/10cm, end with a RS row.
Set-up row (WS) P58 (63, 68, 73, 78), pm, k2, p4, M1, p4, k2, pm, p to end of row—84 (94, 104, 114, 124) sts.

Begin Chart
Row 1 (RS) K13 (18, 23, 28, 33), sm, work row 1 of chart over next 13 sts, sm, k to end.
Row 2 (WS) P58 (63, 68, 73, 78), sm, work row 2 of chart over next 13 sts, p to end.
Cont pats in this way and work armhole shaping same as back until armhole measures 1¾ (2, 2½, 3, 3½)"/4.5 (5, 6.5, 7.5, 9)cm, end with a WS row.

Shape Neck
Next row (RS) Work 24 (29, 34, 39, 44) sts, join a 2nd ball of yarn and bind off center 18 (18, 18, 20, 20) sts, work to end. Working both sides at once with separate balls of yarn, bind off from each neck edge 3 sts once, 2 sts once. Dec 1 st at each neck edge every other row 1 (1, 2, 2, 2) times —18 (23, 27, 31, 36) sts rem each side. Work even until armhole measures same as back. Bind off rem sts each side for shoulder.

SLEEVES
With size 7 (4.5mm) needles, cast on 63 (63, 68, 68, 73) sts. Work in rib for 1½"/4cm, end with a WS row. Beg with a knit (RS) row, work 6 rows in St st (k on RS, p on WS).
Dec row (RS) K1, ssk, k to last 3 sts, k2tog, k1.
Rep dec row every 4th row 3 times more—55 (55, 60, 60, 65) sts.
Work even until piece measures 5"/13cm from beg, end with a WS row.
Inc row (RS) K1, M1, k to last st, M1, k1.
Rep inc row every 4th (4th, 6th, 6th, 6th) row 2 (4, 5, 7, 7) times more—61 (65, 72, 76, 81) sts. Work even until piece measures 12 (12, 12½, 12½, 12½)"/30.5 (30.5, 32, 32, 32)cm from beg.

Shape Cap
Bind off 5 sts at beg of next 2 rows. Dec 1 st each side every other row 5 times, end with a WS row—41 (45, 52, 56, 61) sts. Bind off rem sts.

FINISHING
Block to measurements. Sew shoulder seams.

Neckband
With circular needle and RS facing, pick up and k 100 (105, 110, 115, 120) sts evenly around neck opening. Join and pm for beg of rnd. Work rib in rnds for 1"/2.5cm. Bind off in rib.
Set in sleeves. Sew side and sleeve seams.•

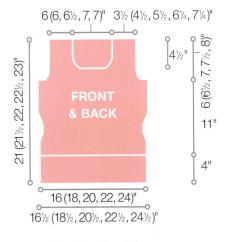

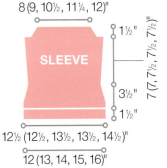

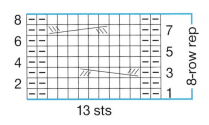

STITCH KEY
☐ k on RS, p on WS
⊟ p on RS, k on WS
▧ 6-st LC
▨ 6-st RC

Bulky Garter Sweater

Easy

SIZES
X-Small/Small (Medium, Large, X-Large/XX-Large). Shown in size Large.

MEASUREMENTS
Bust 38 (42, 47, 51½)"/96.5 (106.5, 119, 131)cm
Length 22 (22½, 23, 23½)"/56 (57, 58.5, 59.5)cm
Upper arm 16 (17, 18, 19½)"/40.5 (43, 45.5, 49.5)cm

MATERIALS
Yarn (6)
Any super bulky alpaca/wool blend, approx 3½oz/100g, 45yd/41m per skein
• 12 (13, 14, 16) skeins in Seafoam

Needles
• One pair each sizes 15 and 17 (10 and 12.75mm) needles, *or size to obtain gauge*
• One size 15 (10 mm) circular needle, 16"/40cm long

Notions
• Stitch holder
• Stitch markers

NOTE
Due to the bulky stitch and weight, fit is determined as oversized.

GAUGE
7 sts and 14 rows to 4"/10cm over garter st using larger needles.
TAKE TIME TO CHECK YOUR GAUGE.

BACK
With smaller needles, cast on 34 (38, 42, 46) sts.
Row 1 (RS) K1 (selvage st), *k2, p2; rep from * to last st, k1 (selvage st).
Row 2 K the knit sts and p the purl sts. Rep rows 1 and 2 for k2, p2 rib for 4 rows more. Change to larger needles.

Begin Garter Stitch Pattern
Note The first and last st of every row forms the decorative selvage sl st.
Row 1 (RS) Sl 1 wyib, k to the last st, k1 tbl.
Row 2 Sl 1 wyif, k to the last st, p1.
Rep rows 1 and 2 until piece measures approx 14½"/37cm from beg.

Shape Armhole
Bind off 2 sts at beg of next 4 rows.
***Dec row (RS)** Sl 1 wyib (selvage st), k2tog, k to the last 3 sts, k2tog, k1 tbl.
Next row (WS) Sl 1 wyif, k to the last st, p1.*
Rep last 2 rows 0 (1, 2, 3) times more—24 (26, 28, 30) sts.
Work even (cont with the sl st selvage st trim) until armhole measures approx 7½ (8, 8½, 9)"/19 (20.5, 21.5, 23)cm. Bind off all sts.

FRONT
Work as for back, including armhole shaping, until armhole measures approx 4 (4½, 5, 5½)"/10 (11.5, 12.5, 14)cm.

Shape Neck
Next row (RS) Work 8 (8, 9, 10) sts, sl center 8 (10, 10, 10) sts to a st holder, join a 2nd ball of yarn and work to end. Working both sides at once with separate balls of yarn, dec 1 st at each neck edge every RS row 3 times—5 (5, 6, 7) sts rem each side.
When armhole measures same as back, bind off rem sts each side for shoulders.

SLEEVES
With smaller needles, cast on 18 (22, 22, 22) sts. Work in k2, p2 rib as on back for a total of 6 rows. Change to larger needles.

Begin Garter Stitch Pattern
Rep rows 1 and 2 as on back for a total of 6 (6, 6, 2) rows.
Inc row (RS) Sl 1 wyib, kfb, k to last 2 sts, kfb, k1 tbl.
Rep inc row every 8th row 5 (4, 5, 6) times more—30 (32, 34, 36) sts.
Work even until piece measures approx 17½"/44.5cm from beg.

Shape Cap
Bind off 2 sts at beg of next 4 rows. Then, rep the 2 dec rows as on back (between *'s) for a total of 4 (5, 6, 7) reps—14 sts. Work even for 4 rows or until cap measures approx 4 (4½, 5, 5½)"/10 (11.5, 12.5, 14)cm. Bind off.

FINISHING
Do *not* block pieces.
Sew shoulder seams. To seam all edges from RS using mattress st, take one half of each selvage st, forming a decorative knit st effect along the edges.

Neckband
With circular needle, pick up and k 44 (48, 48, 48) sts evenly around neck edge, which includes sts on holder for front neck. Join and place marker for beg of rnd. Work in k2, p2 rib for 4 rnds. Bind off in rib.

Sew the sleeves into the armholes. Sew the side and sleeve seams. •

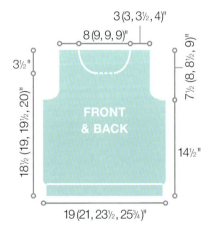

Design Note
The neck shaping on the schematic reflects the FRONT only. The straight edge reflects the top edge of the BACK only.

Classic Raglan Sweater

Intermediate

SIZES
Small (Medium, Large, X-Large, XX-Large). Shown in size Small.

MEASUREMENTS
Bust 37 (40, 44, 48, 52)"/94 (101.5, 111.5, 122, 132)cm
Length 20¼ (21¼, 21¾, 22¾, 23¼)"/51.5 (54, 55, 58, 59)cm
Upper arm 14¼ (14¾, 15½, 16½, 17)"/36 (37.5, 39.5, 42, 43)cm

MATERIALS
Yarn
Any worsted-weight wool, approx 3½oz/100g, 220yd/201m per skein
• 4 (5, 5, 5, 6) skeins in Light Heather Gray (A)
• 1 skein in White (B)

Needles
• One pair each sizes 6 and 7 (4 and 4.5mm) needles, *or size to obtain gauge*

Notions
• Stitch markers
• Stitch holders

GAUGE
20 sts and 27 rows to 4"/10cm over St st using larger needles.
TAKE TIME TO CHECK YOUR GAUGE.

BACK
With smaller needles and B, cast on 93 (101, 111, 121, 131) sts.
Row 1 (RS) K1, *p1, k1; rep from * to end.
Row 2 P1, *k1, p1; rep from * to end.
Rep rows 1 and 2 for k1, p1 rib for 1½"/4cm, end with a WS row. Cut B and join A. Change to larger needles.
With A, work in St st (k on RS, p on WS) until piece measures 11 (11½, 11½, 12, 12)"/28 (29, 29, 30.5, 30.5)cm from beg, end with a WS row.

Shape Armholes
Bind off 3 (4, 6, 8, 10) sts at beg of next 2 rows.
Dec row (RS) K1, k2tog, k to last 3 sts, ssk, k1—2 sts dec'd.
Rep dec row every other row 24 (26, 28, 29, 31) times more—37 (39, 41, 45, 47) sts. Work 1 WS row. Place sts on st holder for back neck.

FRONT
Work as for back to armhole shaping.

Shape Armholes
Bind off 3 (4, 6, 8, 10) sts at beg of next 2 rows.
Dec row (RS) K1, k2tog, k to last 3 sts, ssk, k1—2 sts dec'd.
Rep dec row every other row 18 (20, 22, 23, 25) times more—49 (51, 53, 57, 59) sts. Work 1 WS row. Mark center 23 (25, 27, 31, 33) sts on last row.

Neck Shaping
Dec row (RS) K1, k2tog, k to center marked sts, place center 23 (25, 27, 31, 33) sts on st holder for front neck, join a 2nd ball of A and k to last 3 sts, ssk, k1—12 sts rem each side.
Working both sides at once, cont to work dec's at armhole edge every other row 5 times more, AT THE SAME TIME, dec 1 st at each neck edge every row 3 times, then every other row twice—2 sts rem each side when all shaping is complete. Work 1 WS row.
Next row (RS) K2tog. Fasten off rem st each side.

SLEEVES
With smaller needles and B, cast on 45 (45, 47, 49, 49) sts.
Row 1 (RS) K1, *p1, k1; rep from * to end.
Row 2 P1, *k1, p1; rep from * to end.
Rep rows 1 and 2 for k1, p1 rib for 1½"/4cm, end with a WS row and inc'ing 2 sts evenly across last row—47 (47, 49, 51, 51) sts. Cut B and join A. Change to larger needles.
With A, work in St st (k on RS, p on WS), inc 1 st each side on 9th row, then every 10th (6th, 6th, 6th, 6th) row 2 (2, 6, 15, 16) times, then every 8th (8th, 8th, 0, 0) row 9 (10, 7, 0, 0) times—71 (73, 77, 83, 85) sts. Work even until sleeve measures 17½ (17½, 18, 18, 18½)"/44.5 (44.5, 45.5, 45.5, 47)cm from beg, end with a WS row.

Shape Cap
Bind off 3 (4, 6, 8, 10) sts at beg of next 2 rows.
Dec row (RS) K1, k2tog, k to last 3 sts, ssk, k1—2 sts dec'd.
Work 3 rows even. Rep dec row. Work 1 row even.
Rep last 6 rows 4 (6, 8, 8, 6) times more. Rep dec row on next row, then every other (other, other, other, 4th) row 9 (5, 1, 2, 5) times more—25 sts. Place sts on st holder.

FINISHING
Weave in ends. Block pieces to measurements.
Sew raglan sleeve caps into raglan armholes, leaving back right seam open.

Neckband
With RS facing and smaller needles, k37 (39, 41, 45, 47) sts from back neck holder, 25 sts from left sleeve holder, pick up and k 7 sts along shaped left front neck edge, k23 (25, 27, 31, 33) sts from front neck holder, pick up and k 8 sts along shaped right front neck edge, k25 from right sleeve holder—125 (129, 133, 141, 145) sts.

Design Note
Let your yarn do the talking. This sweater uses a heathered yarn and ribbing in a contrasting color to elevate a classic design.

Classic Raglan Sweater

Boot Toppers

Row 1 (WS) K1,*p1, k1; rep from * to end.
Row 2 P1, *k1, p1; rep from * to end.
Rep rows 1 and 2 twice more, then rep row 1 once more. Bind off loosely in rib.

Sew back right raglan and neckband seam. Sew side and sleeve seams.•

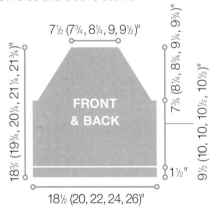

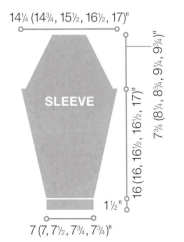

SIZES
X-Small/Small (Medium/Large). Shown in size X-Small/Small.

MEASUREMENTS
Circumference approx 10½ (12)"/ 26.5 (30.5)cm
Length 5½ (6½)"/14 (16.5)cm

MATERIALS
Yarn (4)
Any worsted-weight wool, approx 3½oz/100g, 220yd/201m per skein
• 1 skein each in Light Heather Gray (A), White (B), and Red (C)

Needles
• One pair size 6 (4mm) needles, *or size to obtain gauge*

GAUGE
24 sts and 32 rows to 4"/10cm over k2, p2 rib, slightly stretched, using size 6 (4mm) needles.
TAKE TIME TO CHECK YOUR GAUGE.

BOOT TOPPERS
Lower Edge
With A, cast on 60 (68) sts.
Row 1 (RS) *K1, p1; rep from * to end.
Rep row 1 for k1, p1 rib for 4 rows more.
Row 6 (WS) Rib 5 (1) sts, [M1, k10 (11)] 5 (6) times, M1 (0), rib 5 (1)—66 (74) sts.
Next row (RS) K1, *k2, p2; rep from * to last st, k1.
Next row (WS) K1, *p2, k2; rep from * to last st, k1.
Rep last 2 rows until piece measures 4 (5)"/10 (12.5)cm from beg, end with a WS row.
Cut A, join B.

Top Ribbing
With B, cont in k1, p1 rib for 4 rows.
Join C, and cont in k1, p1 rib for 2 rows.
Rep last 6 rows once more.
With C, bind off all sts in rib.

FINISHING
Sew center back seam. Weave in ends.•

Design Note
If you have enough yarn, it can be fun to make accessories that match your sweater. Boot toppers, hats, cowls, and mittens or gloves are great options.

Hooded or Turtleneck Sweater

Easy

SIZES
Small (Medium, Large, X-Large and XX-Large). Shown in size Small.

MEASUREMENTS
Bust 34½ (37, 39, 43, 47)"/87.5 (94, 99, 109, 119.5)cm
Length 23½ (24, 24½, 25, 25½)"/59.5 (61, 62, 63.5, 64.5)cm
Upper arm 13¼ (14, 14¾, 15½, 16)"/33.5 (35.5, 37.5, 39.5, 40.5)cm

MATERIALS
Yarn 5
Any bulky-weight wool/alpaca/polyamide blend, approx 1¾oz/50g, 115yd/105m per skein
- 7 (7, 8, 9, 9)* skeins in Pink

*Use these amounts if making the hooded version. Use 1 skein less if making the turtleneck version.

Needles
- One pair size 10 (6mm) needles, *or size to obtain gauge*
- One size 10 (6mm) circular needle, 16"/40cm long

Notions
- Stitch holders
- Stitch markers

GAUGE
13 sts and 19 rows to 4"/10cm over St st using size 10 (6mm) needles.
TAKE TIME TO CHECK YOUR GAUGE.

BACK
Cast on 56 (60, 64, 70, 76) sts. Work in St st (k on RS, p on WS) for 5"/12.5cm, end with a WS row.
Dec row (RS) K2, k2tog, k to last 4 sts, ssk, k2—2 sts dec'd.
Rep dec row every 6th row twice more—50 (54, 58, 64, 70) sts.
Work even until piece measures 11½"/29cm from beg, end with a WS row.
Inc row (RS) K2, M1, k to last 2 sts, M1, k2—2 sts inc'd.
Rep inc row every 6th row twice more—56 (60, 64, 70, 76) sts.
Work even until piece measures 15"/38cm from beg, end with a WS row.

Hooded or Turtleneck Sweater

Shape Armholes
Dec row (RS) K2, k2tog, k to last 4 sts, ssk, k2—2 sts dec'd.
Rep dec row every other row 4 (4, 5, 6, 7) times more—46 (50, 52, 56, 60) sts. Work even until armhole measures 7½ (8, 8½, 9, 9½)"/19 (20.5, 21.5, 23, 24)cm, end with a WS row.

Shape Shoulders
Bind off 5 (4, 5, 6, 5) sts at beg of next 2 rows, 4 (5, 5, 5, 6) sts at beg of next 4 rows.
Bind off rem 20 (22, 22, 24, 26) sts.

FRONT
Work as for back until armhole measures 6 (6½, 7, 7½, 8)"/15 (16.5, 18, 19, 20.5)cm, end with a WS row.

Shape Neck
Next row (RS) K16 (17, 18, 19, 20) sts, bind off center 14 (16, 16, 18, 20) sts, join 2nd ball of yarn and k to end. Working both sides at once, purl 1 row.
Dec row (RS) Work to last 4 sts of first side, ssk, k2; on 2nd side, k2, k2tog, k to end—1 st dec'd each side.
Rep dec row every other row twice more, AT THE SAME TIME, when armhole measures same as back to shoulder, shape shoulders as for back by binding off from each shoulder edge 5 (4, 5, 6, 5) sts once and 4 (5, 5, 5, 6) sts twice.

SLEEVES
Cast on 28 (28, 30, 30, 32) sts. Work in St st for 2"/5cm, end with a WS row.
Inc row (RS) K2, M1, k to last 2 sts, M1, k2—2 sts inc'd.
Rep inc row every 8th (8th, 8th, 6th, 6th) row 7 (8, 8, 9, 9) times more—44 (46, 48, 50, 52) sts. Work even until piece measures 17½"/44.5cm from beg, end with a WS row.

Shape Cap
Bind off 2 sts at beg of next 4 rows.
Dec row (RS) K2, k2tog, k to last 4 sts, ssk, k2—2 sts dec'd.
Rep dec row every other row 9 (10, 11, 12, 13) times more. Work 1 WS row. Bind off 2 sts at beg of next 4 rows. Bind off rem 8 sts.

FINISHING
Block pieces lightly to measurements.
Sew shoulder seams.

Option 1: Hood
Cast on 56 (58, 60, 62, 64) sts. Work in St st for 14"/35.5cm. Bind off. Fold in half lengthwise and sew top of hood (bound-off edge) tog.
With RS facing and circular needle, pick up and k 96 sts along face edge of hood.
Row 1 (WS) *P1, k1; rep from * to end.
Cont in k1, p1 rib as established for 1"/2.5cm. Bind off in rib.
Sew hood around neck edge, overlapping by 1"/2.5cm at center front.

Option 2: Turtleneck
With RS facing and circular needle, pick up and k 20 (22, 22, 24, 26) sts along back neck, 11 sts along left front neck edge, 14 (16, 16, 18, 20) sts from front neck holder, and 11 sts along right front neck edge—56 (60, 60, 64, 68) sts. Join and place marker for beg of rnd.
Rnd 1 *K2, p2; rep from * around.
Rep rnd 1 for k2, p2 rib until turtleneck measures 6"/15cm. Bind off in rib.

Set in sleeves. Sew side and sleeve seams. •

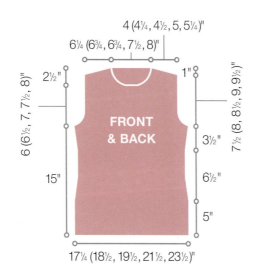
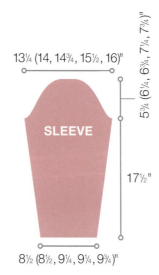

Design Note
Complete this shaped sweater with a turtleneck or a hood. Just follow the instructions for either option in the Finishing section.

Perforated Ridges Sweater

Intermediate

SIZES
Small (Medium, Large, X-Large, XX-Large). Shown in size Small.

MEASUREMENTS
Bust 34 (38, 42½, 46, 50½)"/86.5 (96.5, 108, 117, 128)cm
Length 20 (20½, 21, 21½, 22)"/51 (52.5, 53.5, 55, 56)cm
Upper arm 10¾ (11¾, 13, 15, 16½)"/27.5 (30, 33, 38, 42)cm

MATERIALS
Yarn
- Any DK-weight cotton, approx 2.3oz/65g, 150yd/137m per skein
- 6 (7, 8, 10, 11) skeins in Red

Needles
- One pair size 7 (4.5mm) needles, *or size to obtain gauges*

Notion
- One size G/6 (4mm) crochet hook

GAUGES
- 29 sts and 32 rows to 4"/10cm over k2, p2 rib (slightly stretched) using size 7 (4.5mm) needles.
- 28 sts and 32 rows to 4"/10cm over eyelet rib using size 7 (4.5mm) needles.
TAKE TIME TO CHECK YOUR GAUGES.

K2, P2 RIB
(multiple of 4 sts plus 1)
Row 1 (RS) K1, *p2, k2; rep from * to end.
Row 2 K the knit sts and p the purl sts.
Rep row 2 for k2, p2 rib.

EYELET RIB
(multiple of 4 sts plus 1)
Row 1 (RS) K1, *p3, k1; rep from * to end.
Rows 2–7 K the knit sts and p the purl sts.
Row 8 P1, *k1, yo, k2tog, p1; rep from * to end.
Rep rows 1–8 for eyelet rib.

PATTERN STRIPES
Work 3"/7.5cm in k2, p2 rib.
Work 5"/12.5cm in eyelet rib.
Rep these 8"/20cm for pat stripes.

BACK
Cast on 117 (133, 149, 161, 177) sts. Work in pat stripes for 12½"/32cm.

Shape armhole
Bind off 4 (5, 5, 6, 7) sts at beg of next 2 rows, 2 (2, 3, 3, 3) sts at beg of next 6 rows, 2 sts at beg of next 0 (0, 0, 0, 6) rows. Dec 1 st each side on next row, then every other row 4 (7, 7, 8, 4) times more—87 (95, 105, 113, 123) sts.
Work even in pat stripes until armhole measures 6½ (7, 7½, 8, 8½)"/16.5 (18, 19, 20.5, 21.5)cm, end with a WS row.

Shape Neck
Next row (RS) Work 19 (22, 26, 29, 33) sts, join 2nd ball of yarn and bind off center 49 (51, 53, 55, 57) sts, work to end. Working both sides at once, bind off from each neck edge 3 sts twice. Work even until armhole measures 7½ (8, 8½, 9, 9½)"/19 (20.5, 21.5, 23, 24)cm, end with a WS row. Bind off rem 13 (16, 20, 23, 27) sts each side for shoulders.

FRONT
Work same as for back until armhole measures 4½ (5, 5½, 6, 6½)"/11.5 (13, 14, 15.5, 16.5)cm, end with a WS row.

Shape neck
Next row (RS) Work 28 (31, 35, 38, 42) sts, join 2nd ball of yarn and bind off center 31 (33, 35, 37, 39) sts, work to end. Working both sides at once, bind off from each neck edge 3 sts twice, 2 sts twice, then dec 1 st at each neck edge every other row 5 times.
Work even until armhole measures same as back to shoulder.
Bind off rem 13 (16, 20, 23, 27) sts each side for shoulders.

SLEEVES
Cast on 62 (62, 66, 68, 72) sts.
Next row (RS) K2, *p2, k2; rep from *, end row with k2, (k2, k2, p2, p2).
Cont in k2, p2 rib as established for 9 rows more. Cont in rib and inc 1 st each side

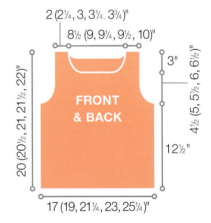

(working inc sts into rib) as foll: [Inc 1 st each side of next row. Work 7 (5, 3, 3, 3) rows even. Inc 1 st each side of next row. Work 9 (5, 5, 3, 3) rows even] 4 (6, 7, 10, 12) times—78 (86, 94, 108, 120) sts.
Work even until piece measures 11 (11½, 12, 12½, 14)"/28 (29, 30.5, 32, 35.5)cm from beg, end with a WS row.

Shape Cap
Bind off 4 (5, 5, 6, 7) sts at beg of next 2 rows, 2 (2, 3, 3, 3) sts at beg of next 6 rows, 2 sts at beg of next 0 (0, 0, 0, 6) rows, dec 1 st each side every other row 10 (13, 14, 14, 13) times, bind off 3 sts at beg of next 4 (4, 4, 8, 8) rows. Bind off rem 26 sts.

FINISHING
Block pieces lightly to measurements.
Sew shoulder seams. With RS facing and crochet hook, work 1 row backwards sc (sc from left to right) evenly around neck edge.
Set in sleeves. Sew side and sleeve seams.
Weave in ends.•

Design Note
Worked in cool cotton and lined with simple eyelets, this sweater is another staple that can be worn year-round.

Chevron Sweater

Intermediate

SIZES
Small (Medium, Large, X-Large).
Shown in size Small.

MEASUREMENTS
Bust 35½ (39, 42, 45¼)"/90 (99, 106.5, 115)cm
Length 23½ (24¼, 25¼, 25½)"/59.5 (61.5, 64, 65)cm
Upper arm 13¼ (14¾, 16½, 18)"/33.5 (37.5, 42, 45.5)cm

MATERIALS
Yarn (4)
Any worsted-weight superwash wool, approx 3½oz/100g, 191yd/175m per skein
• 6 (7, 8, 9) skeins in Green

Needles
• One pair each sizes 6 and 8 (4 and 5mm) needles, *or size to obtain gauge*
• One pair each sizes 6 and 8 (4 and 5mm) circular needles, each 29"/74cm long
• One size 6 (4mm) circular needle, 16"/40cm long
• One set (5) each sizes 6 and 8 (4 and 5mm) double-pointed needles (dpn)

Notions
• Stitch holders
• Stitch markers
• Scrap yarn

GAUGE
20 sts and 28 rows/rnds to 4"/10cm over chevron pat foll chart using larger needles.
TAKE TIME TO CHECK YOUR GAUGE.

NOTE
Pullover is worked by beg with the shoulder edge, then back and front are worked separately to the armhole. Then, pieces are joined to work in rounds for the body and the sleeves are picked up along the armhole edges and worked to the cuffs.

BACK
Right Back Shoulder
With larger needles, cast on 33 (37, 41, 41) sts. Knit 1 row on WS.

Begin chart
Row 1 (RS) Working row 1 or chart, beg with st 1 (5, 1, 1), work to the rep line, then work the 8-st rep 3 (3, 4, 4) times more, end with st 9.
Rows 2–7 Work chart as established. At the end of row 7 (RS), turn work and cast on 23 (23, 23, 31) sts for the neck and lay piece aside.

Left Back Shoulder
Cast on as for right back shoulder and knit 1 row on WS.
Row 1 (RS) Working row 1 of chart, beg with st 1 and work the 8-st rep for 4 (4, 5, 5) reps then work sts 1–4 for 0 (1, 0, 0) time more, end with st 9 (5, 9, 9).
Rows 2–7 Work chart as established.

Join Shoulders
Next row (WS) Work as established on the 33 (37, 41, 41) sts of left back shoulder, cont in pat across the 23 (23, 23, 31) sts for neck, work rem sts in established pat—89 (97,105, 113) sts.
Cont in chevron pat until armhole measures 6¾ (7½, 8½, 8¾)"/17 (19, 21.5, 22)cm.
Leave sts on hold on a strand of scrap yarn.

FRONT
Right Front Shoulder
With larger needles and RS facing, pick up and k 33 (37, 41, 41) sts along cast-on edge of right back shoulder.
Row 2 (WS) Beg with st 9 of chart row 2, work the 8-st rep for 4 (4, 5, 5) reps, end with st 1 (5, 1, 1).
Rows 3–8 Work even foll chart.
Inc row 9 (RS) Work chart to last st, M1 (k or p to keep to pat), k1.
Rep inc row (for neck) every RS row 3 times more—37 (41, 45, 45) sts. Work row 16 of chart. Leave sts on holder.

Left Front Shoulder
With larger needles and RS facing, pick up and k 33 (37, 41, 41) sts along cast-on edge of left back shoulder.
Row 2 (WS) Beg with st 1 of chart row 2, work the 8-st rep for 4 (4, 5, 5) reps, then work sts 1–4 for 0 (1, 0, 0) times more, end with st 9 (5, 9, 9).
Rows 3–8 Work even foll chart.
Inc row 9 (RS) K1, M1 (k or p to keep to pat), work to end.
Rep inc row (for neck) every RS row 3 times more—37 (41, 45, 45) sts. Work row 16 of chart.

Join Shoulders
Next row (RS) Work row 1 of chart over right shoulder sts, cast on 15 (15, 15, 23) sts for center front neck, work across left shoulder sts in pat st—89 (97,105,113) sts. Work chart evenly until there are same number of rows as on back to armhole.

BODY
Note When working the body in rounds, cont to work the pat on each piece, that is in two identical pieces matched at the underarm edges (and not a continuous pat).
Next rnd Work pat across back sts, then work pat across front sts, pm and join to work in rnds—178 (194, 210, 226) sts. Work even until piece measures 15"/38cm from beg.
Change to smaller circular needle and work in k1, p1 rib for 12 rnds.
Bind off using larger needle.

SLEEVES
With larger dpn, pick up and k 66 (74, 82, 90) sts evenly around one armhole. Divide sts onto 4 dpn, work 16 (18, 20, 22) sts on needles 1 and 3 and 17 (19, 21, 23) sts on needles 2 and 4.

Design Note
Just like the Honeycomb Sweater (see pages 16–18), this sweater uses a seamless top-down construction that begins with working each shoulder separately.

Chevron Sweater

Join to work in rnds.
Rnd 1 K1 (selvage st), work the 8-st rep for 7 (8, 9, 10) reps, work sts 9–17.
Work chart evenly for 2"/5cm.
Dec rnd K1, dec 1 st (beg k2tog when first st is a k st or p2tog when st is a p st), work pat to the last 4 sts, dec 1 st (by SKP for a k st or p2tog for a p st), work 1 st, k1.
Rep dec rnd every 8th rnd 8 (9, 11, 12) times more—48 (54, 58, 64) sts.
Work even until sleeve measures 16 (16, 16½, 16½)"/40.5 (40.5, 42, 42)cm from beg.
Change to smaller dpn and work in k1, p1 rib for 12 rnds.
Bind off using larger needle.

FINISHING
Neckband
With shorter circular needle, pick up and k 70 (70, 70, 86) sts around neck edge. Join to work in rnds and pm to mark beg of rnd.
Work in k1, p1 rib for 12 rnds.
Bind off using larger needle.
Lightly block on the WS of piece.•

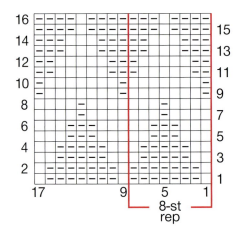

STITCH KEY
☐ k on RS, p on WS
⊟ p on RS, k on WS

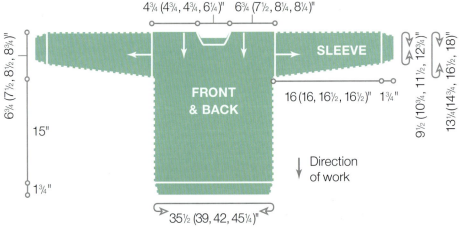